F is for Feathers
A Bird Alphabet

Written by Helen L. Wilbur and Illustrated by Andy Atkins

Parts of a Bird

Neck

Crown

Tail feathers

Eye ring

Beak

Wing bars

Throat

Primary feathers

Breast

Belly

Foot

Claw

Bird Glossary

Avian: having to do with birds

Aviary: a large cage or enclosure for birds

Biodiversity: refers to all the different kinds of life (animals, plants, as well as microorganisms) found in a particular area

Bird-watcher/Birder/Birding: a bird-watcher (also called a birder) is someone who enjoys seeing wild birds. Birding is the act of searching for and seeing wild birds.

Brood: a family of young animals, especially birds

Climate change: changes in the long-term averages of temperature, rainfall, and humidity on a regional or global scale

Conservation: care and protection of natural resources

Cornell Lab of Ornithology: a membership-supported organization at Cornell University dedicated to the understanding and protection of the natural world

Courtship: the process of selecting a mate

Crown: the top of a bird's head

Dispersion: the process of distributing things, like seeds, over a wide area

Ecosystem: a community of living organisms that live and interact with one another in a specific environment

Environment: all the biological, chemical, physical, and cultural factors that surround an organism

Eye ring: a circle of color around a bird's eye that is usually made up of tiny feathers, but is sometimes skin, and is an identifying feature in many birds

Field guide: a book or app for identifying birds, animals, plants, and minerals in the natural environment

Fledgling: a young bird almost ready to leave the nest or recently out of the nest ready to learn to fly and explore its environment. Before a young bird leaves the nest, it is usually called a chick.

Habitat: the natural environment in which a particular organism lives

Hatchling: a bird that has recently hatched from the egg, often called a chick

Invasive species: non-native bird species that takes over food, nesting sites, and territories from native birds

Migration: seasonal movement of birds. Some birds stay in the same place all year, but others travel long distances.

Mobbing: when birds group together to harass or attack a predator

National Audubon Society: a nonprofit organization dedicated to the conservation of birds and their habitat

Nestling: a baby bird developing in the nest and that is dependent on its parents for food

Pollination: transfer of pollen to fertilize plants

Preening: a grooming behavior of birds where they use their beak to clean, strengthen, and position their feathers

Primary feathers: the long feathers on a bird's wing tip, essential for flight

Resident population: birds that stay in the same area year-round rather than migrate

Rookery: a colony of breeding birds, especially herons

Species: a group of animals, plants, or other living things that share common characteristics and can reproduce

Tail feathers: steer and balance a bird and allow it to twist and turn in flight

Wing bars: stripes across a folded wing, useful in bird identification

Birds are amazing and beautiful creatures. They live almost everywhere on earth. Birds are a class of warm-blooded vertebrates called Aves that have two legs, toothless beaks, wings, and feathers, and lay eggs.

There are close to 13,000 species of birds, from the bee hummingbird, which weighs less than a dime, to the ostrich, which can weigh 320 pounds and reach a height of 9 feet. Birds have an incredibly diverse range of sizes, shapes, colors, behaviors, diets, and habitats.

Some birds fly thousands of miles to migrate every year and there are some birds that don't fly at all. They eat many types of foods, including insects, seeds, nectar, fish, fruit, and animals. They live in all types of habitats, from rain forests to the Arctic, from Death Valley to high in the Himalayas.

Birds are a critical part of our ecosystems and maintain biodiversity on our planet. Birds control pests, pollinate plants, disperse seeds, and recycle nutrients back into the earth.

A a

A is for Aves

Into the blue of a sun-filled day,
take to the air and glide away.
Fly high, fly high,
if only I could join you in the sky.

B b

B is for Beak

Catching insects in the air,
cracking nuts and seeds,
sipping nectar, peeling fruit,
beaks show how each bird feeds.

The shape and size of a bird's beak depends on the food it eats. Whether the food is seeds, fish, nectar, insects, or other animals, birds have adapted the perfect beak solution.

Birds that eat seeds, like finches and cardinals, have cone-shaped bills perfect for cracking seeds. The strong hook-shaped beaks of eagles and hawks help them snatch and kill prey. Flycatchers and bee-eaters use their flat, wide beaks to catch insects in flight. Warblers have thin, pointed beaks to pick insects off leaves and bark. Parrots and macaws grab and peel fruit with hooked beaks. Hummingbirds sip nectar with their long strawlike beaks.

Beaks, also called bills, are made of keratin, as are fingernails and turtle shells. Some birds are named for their distinctive beaks, like the roseate spoonbill, shoebill, rhinoceros hornbill, and the sword-billed hummingbird.

Birds use their bills not just for eating, but also for preening (cleaning their feathers), nest building, feeding their young, defending their food or nest, and courting mates.

Chickadees are familiar backyard visitors zipping back and forth to bird feeders. With their cute white-and-black heads, these energetic little birds are easy to enjoy.

Like jays, nuthatches, titmice, and other birds, in order to have food available during the winter months, chickadees store, or *cache*, food. A chickadee may cache hundreds of seeds and insects each day, tucking them neatly into tree bark, pine needles, shingles, or even snow. The trick is to re-find the food when winter comes.

Caching birds have remarkable memories. They use landmarks like rocks and trees to recall the precise locations of hidden food. Plus, they can remember which sites have been emptied. Black-capped chickadees need to live through harsh northern winters. In late summer and fall, their brain size increases in the part that is associated with memory. In the spring, the brain shrinks to normal size.

Their distinctive *chick-a-dee-dee* call gave these birds their name. Chickadees use this call to communicate. To give out a predator alarm, the birds add more *dee* notes to the call. There is a lot going on in these tiny birds.

Cc

C is for Chickadees and Caching

Stopping at the feeder,
 then darting to the trees,
stocking up their winter stash—
 clever chickadees.

D is for Dinosaur

Just think, the hen that
clucks and pecks
is a distant cousin
of the great *T. rex*.

Birds are living dinosaurs. A recent study of *Tyrannosaurus rex* DNA suggests that its closest living relatives are chickens and ostriches. That and fossil evidence seem to confirm that modern birds descended from a group of Jurassic theropod dinosaurs. Those dinosaurs, like the velociraptor, were small, agile predators that walked on their hind legs. However, it took 150 million years for them to evolve into the birds we know today.

Despite their obvious differences, dinosaurs had many features of birds. They had hollow bones, ran on back legs, laid eggs, and, as we now know, many of them had feathers. The first link between birds and dinosaurs was found in 1861 with the discovery of a feathered fossil of a birdlike dinosaur called *Archaeopteryx* (which means "ancient wing"). Since that discovery, many fossils of feathered dinosaurs have been collected and studied.

Birds had to become smaller to fly for long periods of time. The shortened front legs of the theropod became wings and the avian ancestors went from gliding to true flight.

Dd

E e

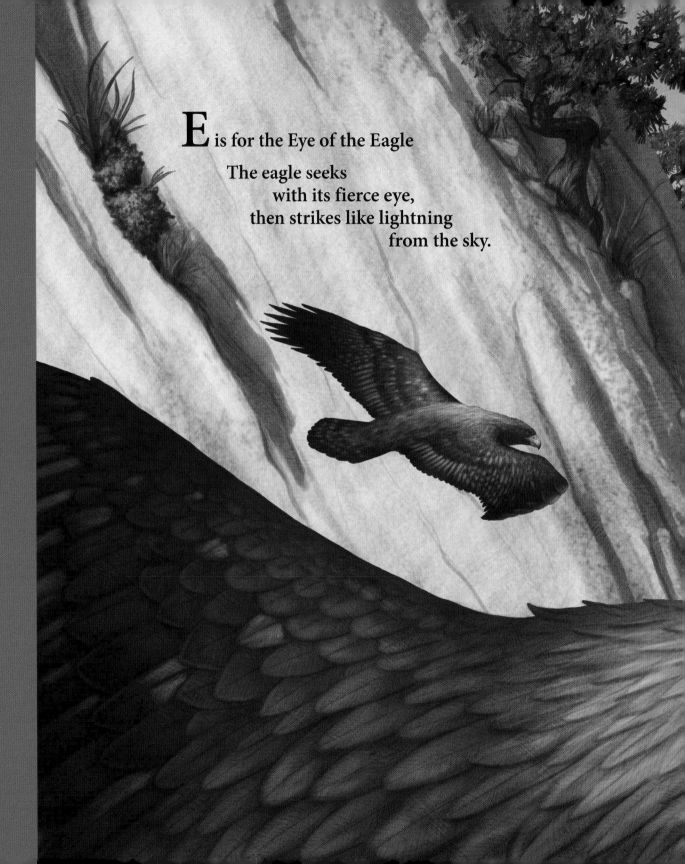

E is for the Eye of the Eagle

The eagle seeks
with its fierce eye,
then strikes like lightning
from the sky.

An eagle can spot a rabbit from more than a mile away. Like all birds, an eagle's vision is its most important sense. Birds need excellent vision to find food, catch fast-moving prey, escape from predators, and navigate in flight without colliding.

Birds have exceptional eyesight. They have two to eight times the number of visual cells than the human eye, as well as larger eyes relative to their size. An eagle, which may weigh 10 pounds, has the same size eyes as a human. Many birds have eyes on the sides of their heads that allow them to see sideways as well as forward. This gives the American woodcock a 360-degree field of vision. Recently, scientists have found evidence that birds have an eye protein that can detect the earth's magnetic field, which helps orient them in flight and navigate long-distance migration.

Birds also have amazing color vision. Humans have three color receptors, for blue, green, and red. Our cats and dogs have only two. But birds have a fourth for ultraviolet light, which opens for them a world of color invisible to us.

F is for Feathers

Soft and bright, strong and light,
perfectly designed for flight,
for keeping warm and dry and sleek,
feathers make all birds unique.

Birds are the only animal with feathers. Feathers allow birds to fly, swim, and stay insulated. Together with size and shape, the feathers, their color and pattern, give each species its distinct appearance. Feathers are made of keratin, like a bird's beak and human fingernails. Birds have different types of feathers for different purposes. Tail, wing, and body feathers are called contour feathers. They give a bird shape and the ability to fly. Wing and tail feathers steer and control flight. Down feathers, which are fluffy and close to a bird's body, keep it warm and dry.

A bird's number of feathers depends on its size and environment. The tundra swan, which breeds in the Arctic and winters on the Atlantic and Pacific coasts of North America, has more than 25,000 feathers. Small songbirds have just 1,500 to 3,000 feathers.

Birds preen their feathers to clean and repair them. Feathers wear out and need to be replaced. Birds shed their feathers once or twice a year in a process called molting. This is usually a gradual change so the bird can still fly, as new feathers grow and push out the old ones.

Ff

A bird's geographic range is the area where the species lives and is found. Many species have large ranges, though an individual of the species may only live and thrive in a small territory within the species' range. Great horned owls are found throughout North America, but a nesting pair may spend their lives within just a 25-mile area. A ruffed grouse may live on just five or six acres. The arctic tern nests in the Arctic Circle and migrates to Antarctic seas, and then back again each year.

Migrating birds have different breeding and wintering grounds, as well as migratory routes and locations where they settle year-round. The whimbrel, a brown-and-white shorebird, breeds in the Arctic and winters as far as the southern tip of South America. Egrets have both resident and migrating populations. Once hunted nearly to extinction for their beautiful plumage, egrets have recovered and are now expanding their range and population in North America.

Species found only in a specific zone and not anywhere else are referred to as *endemic* to that area. Carolina chickadees have a sizeable range but are still endemic to the United States. While McKay's buntings, found only on a few islands in the Bering Sea, are endemic to Alaska.

Gg

G is for Geographic Range

Some bird species travel far,
many stay right where they are.
Birds live where it suits them best
for food and shelter, a place to rest.

H h

H is for Habitat

Egrets raise their fluffy chicks
in nests out on a limb
right above the waters
where alligators swim.

Birds have adapted to nearly every habitat on earth. A habitat is the natural environment where an organism lives that provides the food, shelter, and water it needs to survive. Some major habitats are forests, deserts, grasslands, mountain and polar regions, and water.

Wetlands, such as marshes, bayous, and swamps, are areas where water covers the earth for all or part of the year. Wetlands support rich plant and animal life, making them great habitats for all types of birds.

Wading birds like egrets, ibises, wood storks, and herons are specifically adapted for wetland habitats. Long legs keep their feathers dry as they wade through shallow water. Long toes support them in mud and wet sand. Long necks let them strike into the water with their daggerlike beaks to catch food.

Wetland birds regularly nest together in large rookeries in trees over waters that are often home to healthy alligator populations. Alligators act as natural guardians by preying on the raccoons, possums, and snakes that might otherwise climb up and eat bird eggs or babies.

I i

I is for Incubation

Mother mallard
leads her brood
to the pond to swim
and hunt for food.

Eggs need warmth in order for the embryos inside to grow into baby birds. Almost all birds warm their eggs by incubation, which means sitting on them and using the warmth of their bodies to keep the eggs at an even temperature. The length of the incubation period depends on the size of the bird. Small songbirds hatch in a couple of weeks, while large albatrosses can take 80 days.

In most species, both bird parents share incubation and parenting duties. The babies are called hatchlings for their first few days out of the shell.

Hatchlings grow to become nestlings. As they grow feathers for flight, the babies develop into fledglings ready to venture into the world. Bird babies get lots of help and protection from their parents as they grow. When baby songbirds leave the nest, the parents stay nearby to watch over their chicks. Mother ducks bring their young to water very soon after hatching to swim and feed. The ducklings will stay close to her for a couple of months.

Blue jays are sometimes unfairly criticized for their behavior in the backyard. These bold, bright birds are often considered bullies around the feeder because they cause a ruckus and chase away other birds. Jays, ravens, crows, and magpies belong to the corvid family of birds. Corvids can be loud and annoying and are treated as nuisance birds. But cross them at your peril. Crows can remember your face and they carry grudges.

Corvids, especially crows and ravens, have long had the reputation of being sly and clever, but recent research has uncovered how smart these birds really are. They solve problems, make and use tools, plan ahead, and appear to have the reasoning of a seven-year-old human.

Researchers found that crows recognize faces and associate them with both positive and negative feelings. The crows not only pestered people who treated them badly, they also told their friends and families about them. Scientists aren't yet sure how they do this. However, don't worry: crows also remember kindness and are known to bring gifts to those who treat them well.

Jj

J is for Jays

Strutting toward the feeder,
flashing feathers blue,
    the jays are here for breakfast,
a bold and noisy crew.

Not all birds fly in the air. There are nearly 60 species of flightless birds throughout the world.

Penguins live in the Southern Hemisphere, from Antarctica to the Galápagos Islands at the equator. King penguins are the largest penguins outside of Antarctica. While clumsy on land, penguins are strong and graceful swimmers. Instead of wings, penguins have flippers that propel them through water and make them excellent underwater hunters. King penguins can dive to more than 1,000 feet and can stay underwater for more than five minutes, giving them plenty of time to find and catch fish.

Many flightless birds belong to a group called ratites, which includes the ostrich, emu, and kiwi. The kiwi, a national symbol of New Zealand, is a pear-shaped bird with a long beak, tiny wings, and no tail. The kiwi lived on an island with no predators until humans arrived 1,000 years ago. Scientists theorize that's why it didn't need to fly. Its cousins, the ostrich, emu, and cassowary, are among the world's largest birds. They have long, powerful legs and use their wings to steer when running.

K is for King Penguins and Kiwis

While it's true that penguins don't fly in the air,
to say they're flightless is not really fair.
When they dive in the water, all the fish flee.
The fact is that penguins can fly in the sea.

Kk

L is for Lovebirds

Preening feathers with great care,
    locking talons in midair,
dancing on the quiet pond,
    birds renew their lifetime bond.

L l

Lovebirds are colorful little parrots that, like mute swans, whooping cranes, Atlantic puffins, and other birds, are known to mate for life. Lovebirds got their name because they form especially strong pair-bonds. Most bird species stick to one partner, but only for a nesting, a season, or several seasons. Strong partner bonds contribute to the stability of flocks and the success in raising young birds.

Building a bird family begins with courtship. In the spring, male birds attract females with behavior as simple as a song or as extravagant as an elaborate mating dance. A blue-footed booby gets the party started by showing off his bright blue feet, taking a bow with wings extended, and offering a twig to his prospective mate. Sandhill crane pairs perform a ballet that involves jumping, bowing, and wing flapping. Western grebes dance across the surface of the water. Eagles and hawks perform acrobatic aerial displays, flying, plunging, and locking talons.

Bonded pairs reestablish their partnership with courtship rituals each mating season or after a separation. Pairs strengthen their bond by feeding each other, preening, nest building, and other activities.

Birds migrate in order to survive. As winter comes to northern regions where birds breed, sources of food, like nectar and insects, begin to disappear. Birds start to fly south in flocks to find food in warmer climates. As spring approaches, the birds return to their breeding grounds. Here they can raise their young where there is more space and less competition for food. An estimated 40 percent of birds make a migration journey.

Birds in mountainous areas may simply migrate to different altitudes, but other birds travel amazing distances. The arctic tern migrates from the Arctic Circle to the Antarctic Circle—that's a yearly journey of more than 25,000 miles! Migration is a massive feat of endurance and a very dangerous time for birds. Storms, predators, starvation, and exhaustion all threaten birds during their journey.

M
m

M is for Migration

Millions of birds in the dark of the night
winging by overhead as we sleep,
guided by stars and the setting sun
over rivers and valleys they sweep.

Migrating birds often remember and return to where they were born. Even on their first migration, birds can find their southern wintering grounds on their own. How do they do this? Scientists don't know for sure. Some of it is instinct, but we do know that birds use a combination of the sun, stars, the earth's magnetic field, natural landmarks, and smell to find their way.

Many migratory birds fly at night to avoid predators, but hummingbirds travel during the day. In order to bulk up for the long trip, hummingbirds gain 25 to 40 percent of their normal body weight. These little birds require a lot of energy to flap their wings 20 to 80 times per second. Most North American hummingbirds migrate to Mexico or Central America for the winter, which means that some ruby-throated hummingbirds need to fly 18 to 20 hours nonstop over the Gulf of Mexico. That's a huge effort for such a tiny bird.

N n

Down on the ground, high in the trees, in cliffs or burrows or a cavity in a tree, on the ledge of a building, or maybe in a birdhouse in your backyard—that's where you can find birds nesting to bring up their young. Twigs, leaves, hair, grass, pine needles, mud, saliva, clay, and many other things provide the building materials for nests. What's more incredible is that every species of bird knows when and what particular type of nest it needs to build. However, the purpose of building any nest is the same: to provide a warm and safe home for babies to hatch, grow, and stay out of the way of predators.

For years, bluebirds were threatened by loss of nesting sites. Fortunately, bluebirds take to nesting in man-made wooden boxes. A single nest box can attract bluebirds to your yard. Bluebird lovers have taken this a step further and have created carefully spaced trails ranging from just a few to a couple of thousand nesting boxes, helping the birds to make a comeback. Check to see if there is a bluebird trail near you.

N is for Nests

Come along the bluebird trail,
　　nesting boxes in a row.
Safe and warm in cozy homes,
　　little baby bluebirds grow.

O is for Ornithologists

Be a naturalist, biologist,
park ranger, ornithologist.
It isn't just for nerds—
it's cool to study birds!

If you like wildlife and being outdoors, becoming an ornithologist may be right for you. Ornithologists are scientists who study birds. The word comes from the Latin roots of *ornis* (bird) and *logos* (science or thought). You need to have a college or advanced degree in biology, wildlife biology, zoology, ecology, or related fields of study. And there's a lot more to it than looking at birds.

Ornithologists work in many settings. They can be park rangers, land managers, outdoor educators, researchers, ecologists, or teachers at colleges and universities. Aviaries and zoos employ them to maintain and preserve captive bird populations. Ornithologists do research at government agencies, nonprofits, and academic institutions. Ornithologists may work in the field conducting research, as outdoor educators, or leading tours for bird lovers.

Not all work is outside. Computer programming has a central role in monitoring and following worldwide bird populations, as well as in developing techniques for the classification of birdsongs.

Oo

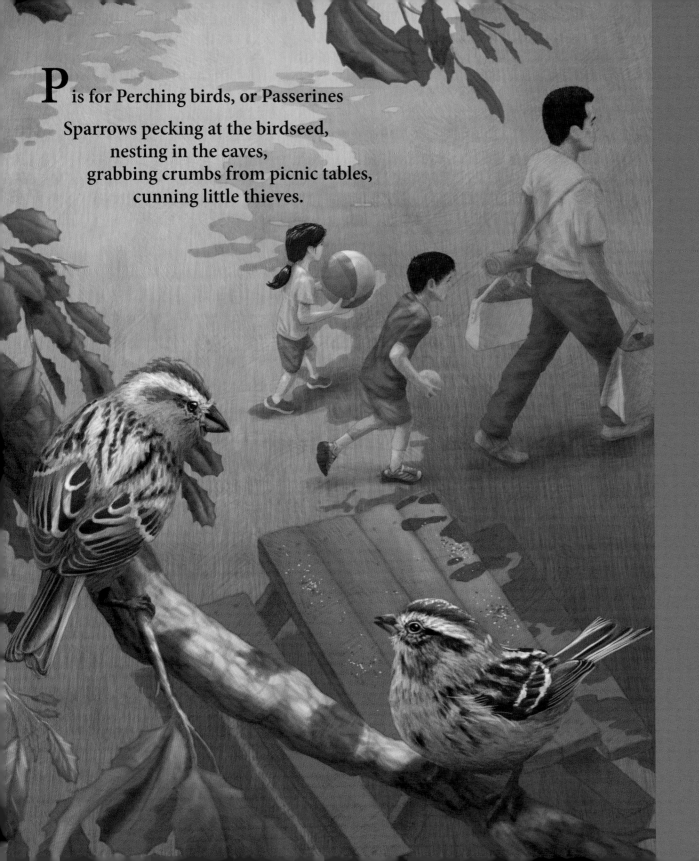

P is for Perching birds, or Passerines

Sparrows pecking at the birdseed,
nesting in the eaves,
grabbing crumbs from picnic tables,
cunning little thieves.

Pp

Perching birds, or passerines, make up 60 percent of the world's bird species. Passerines have three toes pointing forward and one backward, perfect for grasping and perching on branches, a wire, or your feeder. Many familiar birds, such as robins, cardinals, wrens, finches, and orioles, are passerines.

Passerines tend to be small to midsize birds. Many passerines are also songbirds. The bird's vocal organ is called the syrinx. Songbirds, like thrushes, meadowlarks, and nightingales, have a particularly well-developed syrinx that helps them produce complex and musical songs.

The term *passerine* comes from the Latin word for *sparrow*, which refers to what is known today as the house sparrow. A bird of city streets, backyards, or small farms, since the first farming settlements appeared in the Middle East about 11,000 years ago, the sparrow has prospered across Europe and Asia, always living near people. In 1851, a bird lover brought eight pairs from London to Brooklyn, New York, and released them. Today about 25 million live in the United States and Canada. House sparrows are an example of an invasive species in North America.

All of the feathers on a bird, their pattern, shape, and color, make up its plumage. The color and pattern of plumage are key factors in bird identification. However, a single species may have different types of plumage. In some species, like the blue jay, both male and female birds look the same. But in others, like northern cardinals, the male and female look different.

The most spectacular plumage is on display during mating season. As female birds often do the choosing, the males have developed brighter plumage to attract them. Found in the tropical forests of Central America, the quetzal (ket-ZAL) has vibrant plumage of green, red, and blue, making it one of the world's most beautiful birds. Each spring, the male quetzals sprout twin tail feathers, up to three feet long, to entice mates.

The plumage of hatchlings and young birds may go through several stages before the adult, or basic plumage, stage. Many birds, especially young ones, have plumage that blends into the environment to hide them from predators. The plumage of the eastern screech owl makes it almost impossible to see against tree bark.

Qq

Q is for Quetzal

The quetzal in its emerald green
sits among the leaves unseen.
Little screech owls, light and dark,
blend right in with wood and bark.

R r

Owls and ospreys, like falcons, eagles, kites, and hawks, are raptors, or birds of prey. Raptors are predators that kill other animals for food. They have excellent eyesight, strong hooked beaks, and sharp claws called talons, all designed to locate, grasp, and kill prey. Most raptors hunt during the day for small mammals and reptiles. But owls and ospreys have special adaptations.

Owls hunt at night. Their huge eyes help them see well in low light. But owls can capture prey by sound alone. The circle of feathers around an owl's face acts like a satellite dish, directing sound to the ear openings on the sides of its head. (The "ear" tufts on top of an owl's head are not ears but display feathers.) And, because of its special wing feathers, owls have the unique advantage of silent flight.

Ospreys feed primarily on fish. Ospreys perch or hover over water, then dive headfirst when they spot a fish. Seconds before they hit the water, they shift position, putting their talons first to snatch their prey. Ospreys have a reversible outer toe perfect for grasping a slippery fish.

R is for Raptors

Deep in the woods
  in the dark of the night,
watch as the owl
  like a shadow takes flight.

Close to sunrise is the best time to hear birds sing. Birds greet the new day with a birdsong symphony known as the dawn chorus. Most birds produce short, simple call notes to signal danger, make contact, ask for food, or say, "Here I am." Birdsongs have longer, complex patterns. Mostly male birds sing to mark their territory or attract a mate.

Baby birds learn the songs from their parents. They listen and imitate the vocalizations until they get them right. Some birds, like tyrant flycatchers, have songs that they inherit and do not learn. Birds can do extraordinary vocal feats. The northern cardinal can sing more notes than there are on a piano. The wood thrush can sing two notes at the same time. Brown thrashers have a large repertoire with more than 1,000 sounds. They're mimics, like mockingbirds and catbirds.

The loon, a black-and-white waterbird, is known for its beautiful calls. Loon pairs check on one another with long, high wails that echo across a lake. Single-note hoots reassure chicks, while wavy calls signal distress. Once you've heard the haunting sound, you won't forget it.

S s

S is for Songs and Calls

The song of the thrush in the meadow,
    the call of the loon on the lake,
the cheerful sound of the robin
        as the world begins to wake.

T is for Threats

Protect our wildlife, natural places,
  woods and oceans, open spaces.
Help all species to survive,
   give our birds a place to thrive.

Tt

Birds are an essential part of our ecosystems. The health of bird populations is a major indicator of the health of our environment. Birds are very sensitive to environmental changes. Climate change and loss of habitat are among the greatest threats to bird survival; they cause disruptions in food sources and bird migration. Every year, millions of acres of bird-friendly land are lost to development, industrial farming, and logging. Millions of birds are also killed by outdoor pet cats and by flying into windows. The city of Philadelphia has started to dim its skyline at night to save birds that fly through on their annual migration.

Conservation groups are fighting back. The Endangered Species Act protects species and their habitats. Captive breeding saved the California condor from extinction. In 1987, the species was down to 27 individuals. In 1992, the program began to reintroduce condors to the wild. Today more than 500 California condors exist in captivity and the wild. Bird and wildlife conservation agencies work to restore habitats, relocate species, and support legislation that protects birds.

When birds rise high above the earth, wings outstretched and motionless, circling slowly, higher and higher, they are soaring. How can they fly so long and effortlessly without flapping their wings?

Columns of warm air, called thermals, rise off the ground as they're heated by sunlight. Birds soar by using their wings to push air downward, creating an updraft, which keeps them up and enables them to fly using very little energy. Birds fly in a spiral within the thermals, riding them to higher altitudes. Birds can glide from thermal to thermal, traveling over many miles. Soaring flight assists birds during long migrations, allowing them to conserve the energy needed to travel long distances.

Seabirds that travel over vast stretches of ocean are masters at soaring flight. Albatrosses are large oceangoing birds with the longest wingspan of any living animal, more than 11 feet. They spend the first six years of their lives over the ocean and can cover 10,000 miles in a single journey. The oldest bird tracked by scientists is a Laysan albatross named Wisdom who is more than 70 years old.

U is for Updraft

Upward rising, smooth and slow,
circle round the earth below.
Ride the currents, calm and still,
soar above the field and hill.

Uu

A familiar sight in the autumn sky is migrating geese flying south in a V-shaped formation. Why do they do it? The birds coordinate their wing flapping to catch the updraft of the birds ahead. This saves vital energy and reduces fatigue on long migratory flights.

Starlings are known for flocking together in a huge swirling mass called a murmuration. Thousands of starlings twist and swoop across the evening sky in ever-changing patterns. Scientists continue to study this phenomenon to understand how and why the birds move in these synchronized patterns.

Birds gather together for many reasons. When flying or foraging, there is safety in numbers—more birds to detect predators and to find food. A large group of birds can mob a predator to scare it away. Birds, particularly seabirds, nest in large colonies to provide better chances of survival for their chicks. One of the largest colonies is in Scotland on Bass Rock, where 150,000 northern gannets gather to nest. The gannets have been using this spot as a rookery since the fifteenth century.

V v

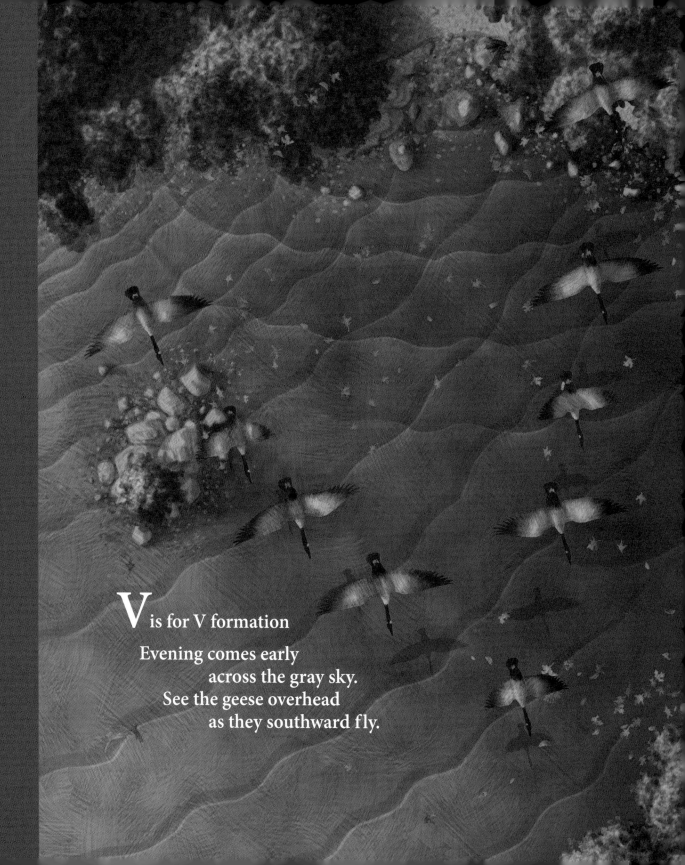

V is for V formation

Evening comes early
          across the gray sky.
See the geese overhead
          as they southward fly.

W is for Wings

Fringed with feathers, stretched in flight,
flutter, hover, dive, or fight,
built for speed or gliding high,
wings lift birds into the sky.

Birds' bodies evolved for flight with their lightweight, hollow bones; feathers; a streamlined shape like an arrow; and wings. Flying requires an upward motion called *lift* and a forward push called *thrust*. Birds that fly use strong breast muscles to flap their wings. As the wings push on the air, the air moves the bird forward, producing thrust. Wings are shaped larger in front and are curved on top. The air on the top moves faster over the wing. The slower air on the bottom has a higher air pressure and will move the wing up, creating lift.

Wings have different sizes and shapes and are adapted to a bird's size and way of life. Soaring and gliding require long wings. Smaller wings allow birds to move quickly through trees and to rapidly change direction.

The fastest bird—in fact, the fastest animal in the world—is the peregrine falcon. Its pointed wings help it to reach speeds of 40 to 60 miles per hour during flight. However, when the bird makes its high-speed hunting dive, it can reach 200 miles per hour. That is a deadly dive.

W
W

For more than a century, the National Audubon Society has conducted a Christmas Bird Count, relying on the dedication of volunteer birders. One of the great joys of birding is the opportunity for ordinary citizens to contribute to science and bird conservation. Whether you are a newbie or an expert, all are welcome. And you can do it right in your neighborhood or backyard. Get out your binoculars and bird guide and sign up at audubon.org.

The Christmas Bird Count provides an early winter bird census, or total number. The data collected helps scientists evaluate the health of bird populations and guides conservation efforts in the Western Hemisphere.

Each February, the National Audubon Society teams up with the Cornell Lab of Ornithology for the Great Backyard Bird Count. Participants can count the birds they see and then enter the results online. This is a four-day worldwide event involving hundreds of thousands of participants from more than 100 countries. You can join in for as little as 15 minutes to help the birds you see every day.

X is for Xmas Bird Count

Take your binoculars
    and look outside.
What bird is that?
    Check your guide.

Y is for Your Yard

To see the wonder of birds,
you don't have to go far.
Just look out your window
and there they are.

You can enjoy birds almost anywhere, whether you live in the center of a city or are hiking in a forest. Here's how to get started: Get outside and look up. Your backyard, local parks, gardens, riverbanks, and beaches are great places to find birds as well as quiet settings to enjoy them. Go with a friend or see if there is a local bird club that sponsors bird walks.

Get a bird guide at your library or bookstore so that you can start identifying and learning about the birds that you might see in your area. Your phone or computer is a great resource. Invest in or borrow an inexpensive pair of binoculars to see birds more clearly and up close. Take a photo or sketch the birds you see. What do they look like? Where are they? What are they doing? Don't ignore common birds like pigeons or gulls—they have more interesting lives than you might think.

Bird-watchers, also called birders, are eager to share their love of birds, so don't be afraid to ask for help. You might make some new friends.

Z is for Zones

It's spring along the river—
     warm air brings the rains.
From the southern skies we hear
     the wingbeats of the cranes.

Flyway zones are the migratory routes that birds follow as they travel between their northern breeding and southern wintering grounds. There are four north-south flyway zones in North America. Coastlines form the Atlantic and Pacific flyways. The Central covers the Great Plains and the Rocky Mountains. The Mississippi flyway follows the 2,530-mile-long Mississippi River.

Hungry and tired birds rest and refuel at certain locations, called stopover sites, during their migratory journey. Birds often use the same sites year after year. The coasts of Louisiana; Cape May, New Jersey; and San Francisco Bay are well-known sites. Every spring, the Platte River in Nebraska offers a rest stop for more than 500,000 migrating sandhill cranes. These birds stop on their journey for food, shelter, and rest along the river. Over 250 other species use this location on the Central flyway. Bird lovers come from all over the world to witness this magnificent spectacle.

You can consult BirdCast online to discover which migrating birds will go through your area. Keep your feeders full and clean and offer fresh water for the birds on their long journey.

Z z

How to Help the Bird World!

Habitat loss and climate change threaten birds. These issues may seem overwhelming and beyond your control, but you can take small but powerful steps to preserve and help the birds around you. The good news is that protecting birds also protects us.

Here are some suggestions on how to get started:

- Create a backyard or balcony sanctuary. Whether you have a window box, a small patio, or a big yard, you can make it a welcome stop or home for birds. Use native (local to your area) plants and bushes to attract birds. Native plants will also bring butterflies and bees. Local nurseries, garden clubs, and botanical gardens, as well as online resources, can provide ideas for the best plants for your area. Researchers have discovered that biodiversity adds to human happiness. You will be building a sanctuary for yourself as well as for birds.

- Put up a bird feeder. Providing food attracts birds to your yard. Birds have different feeding habits. Find out what type of birds are in your neighborhood and get the type of feeder and food for them. Having birds in your yard brings a summer bonus: They eat lots of insects in addition to the seeds you provide.

- Don't forget the water. Birds need clean water for drinking and bathing. Few things are more fun than watching visiting birds maintain their feathers by splashing around in a birdbath.

- Don't feed bread to birds. Bread is not a natural food source for birds. It has relatively low nutritional value, providing no protein or fat. Seeds, nectar, insects, suet, and fruit and vegetable leaves and peelings are all better choices.

- Cats are predators of birds and kill millions of them each year. Indoor cats live longer than cats that are allowed outside, where they pick up diseases, get hit by cars, or become food for other animals. The only way to keep your cat from killing birds is to keep it indoors. Collars with bells don't work, as birds do not associate the sound of a bell with danger. Domesticated cats live happy and fulfilling lives in the house. Practice responsible cat ownership.

- Add a birdhouse to your yard. By providing a nesting box, you'll experience the joy of watching birds build their nests, create a family, and launch their young into life.

- Participate in a bird count. Get to know the birds and fellow bird lovers in your area.

**Enjoy the peace and beauty of the birds and nature around you.
You'll be developing a hobby you can enjoy for a lifetime.**

What Type of Bird Is That?

Train yourself to be a bird detective. Watch, listen, and learn. Watching birds is great training for observation. Exploring the world of birds gives you skills of patience, observation, and evaluation that help with other pursuits.

But how do you figure out what type of bird you are looking at?

Start with a list of birds that are common to your area. See if you can find them in your yard or while you are walking around your neighborhood. There are lots of good bird guides for your area. The National Audubon Society, the Cornell Lab of Ornithology, and many other organizations have websites and apps for identifying birds.

Here's what to look for:

Size and shape: Is it as small as a chickadee, bigger like a robin or crow, or larger still like a heron? Is it plump, sleek? What is the shape of its beak? Its feet?

Color pattern: Look at the overall color pattern on its head, wings, and chest.

Behavior: What was it doing? Soaring in the sky, skimming the surface of the water, wading along a lagoon, visiting your bird feeder, hopping on the ground . . .

Habitat: Where did you see it? In a marsh, on a riverbank, at the seashore, soaring high in the sky, in the woodlands, the desert, or deep in the bushes? Both the general area and the exact site of the bird are big clues.

You can sketch your sighting or take a photo for later verification.

Some other things to think about as you learn how to be a bird-watcher:

- Dress appropriately—wear comfortable clothes and shoes or boots suitable for the outdoor environment. Be ready for rain. Don't forget to put a hat, sunblock, water, and insect spray in your backpack.

- Be patient, keep your distance, and allow the bird to show itself.

- Keep a low profile, keep your sound low, don't shuffle or drag your feet, and keep your movements slow, not sudden. You don't want to startle the bird.

Respect the environment, the wildlife around you, and other birders you may meet.

To Wesley and Toni, Dedria and Alex, and forever for Chris
—Helen

To Kurt, for whose friendship and guidance I will always be grateful.
—Andy

Sleeping Bear Press and author Helen L. Wilbur wish to thank and acknowledge George L. Armistead, an associate at the Academy of Natural Sciences of Drexel University and co-founder of BirdPhilly.org, for his expertise in reading and reviewing the manuscript. Special thanks also to Victoria McMillan, associate professor of writing–natural sciences, research associate, biology, emerita, Colgate University, and Robert Arnold, professor of biology, emeritus, Colgate University.

SLEEPING BEAR PRESS™
2395 South Huron Parkway, Suite 200
Ann Arbor, MI 48104
www.sleepingbearpress.com

Printed and bound in the United States.

10 9 8 7 6 5 4 3 2 1

Library of Congress Cataloging-in-Publication Data

Names: Wilbur, Helen L., 1948- author. | Atkins, Andy, 1958- illustrator.
Title: F is for feathers : a bird alphabet / written by Helen L. Wilbur ; and illustrated by Andy Atkins. Description: Ann Arbor, MI : Sleeping Bear Press, [2022]. | Series: Alphabet | Audience: Ages 6-10. | Summary: "Following the alphabet, poetry and sidebar text explore all aspects of bird life, from identification to habitat to how to be a bird watcher. Includes a glossary"—Provided by publisher.
Identifiers: LCCN 2021037466 | ISBN 9781534111400 (hardcover) Subjects: LCSH: Birds—Juvenile literature. | English language—Alphabet—Juvenile literature. | Alphabet books. | LCGFT: Alphabet books. | Picture books.
Classification: LCC QL676.2 .W535 2022 | DDC 598—dc23
LC record available at https://lccn.loc.gov/2021037466